THE
POWER
OF THE
SEED

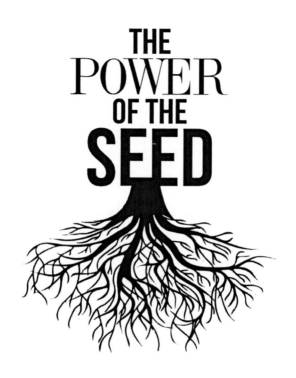

THE
POWER
OF THE
SEED

DR ERIC L. HOLMES

purposely created
PUBLISHING

Special discounts are available on bulk quantity purchases by book clubs, associations and special interest groups. For details email:
sales@publishyourgift.com
or call (888) 949-6228.

For information logon to:
www.PublishYourGift.com

This book is truly in honor of my mother Ernestine Folks Holmes who transitioned on January 7, 2015. I will always cherish and honor the values she instilled in me.

TABLE OF CONTENTS

Dedication.. v

Acknowledgements 9

Introduction 11

PART I: SOWING YOUR SEED

    Biblical Testaments 27

    Hear, Model, and Teach God's Word 35

    Worship in Giving...42

    Equate Your Name with Excellence...............................45

    Expect a Harvest 50

PART II: NURTURING YOUR SEED

    Be Patient 60

    Be Not Weary...61

    Get into Position..63

    Know Who You Are..66

PART III: HARVESTING YOUR SEED

    Rejoice in Favor 78

    Keep Going..81

Conclusion 83

About the Author 87

To Pau, Pau,

I am You

Dr. E

ACKNOWLEDGEMENTS

First, I give thanks and glory to God just for allowing me to write this book, as it was birthed out of an experience and word. I am eternally appreciative.

To my family, friends, and church family who support and love me.

To a great pastor, the late Apostle R. Evans, who poured so much good into my life and spoke such words of wisdom.

To the best pastor and mentor, Bishop R. Pender, my life has been enriched and enhanced because of you.

To Dr. P. Pender, Lady B. Bragg, and Lady W. Evans, thank you all for such great gifts of wisdom.

To my coworker, Captain, who helped structure and steer me in the right direction, I thank you for all of your help.

To Dr. B. Lawrence for your prayers, support, love, and wisdom; you pulled a lot out of me for my purpose.

To my sister, P. Cox, the rock of my family, words cannot express my love.

To everyone, thank you for everything.

<u>INTRODUCTION</u>

I was inspired and led by God to write this book, which has been birthed in me for some time now. During one of my sermons on the prayer line for Freshwater Ministries, I set out to enlighten believers on the power of their seed when it is sown properly. God led me to Isaiah 55:10, and the verse spoke to me in a way that it never had before.

For as the rain cometh down, and the snow
from heaven, and returneth not thither,
but watereth the earth, and maketh it
bring forth and bud, that it may give seed
to the sower, and bread to the eater.

(Isaiah 55:10 King James Version)

In agriculture, every plant begins with a seed. A seed that is sown under the right conditions will produce a means of life for the consumer. It is the same for the believer. When we sow under the right conditions, we can expect God to bless the seed, and we will reap a harvest in our due season. When believers understand the concept of seedtime and harvest, they will know that every harvest in their lives started with a seed.

I have sown and planted my seed for many years, and I have seen the manifestation come to pass. My life is enriched and blessed because of the awesome teachings I have received, which began with my mother. She instilled that tenacious spirit in each of her eight children, along with integrity, character, prayer, and the love of God. She would tell us to always help others whenever we could. Even in death, she upheld this tenet by donating her body to the Penn State Hershey Medical Center to help find a cure for multiple sclerosis.

I took all that she taught, directly and indirectly, and applied it to my life. I have a passion for helping people, personally and professionally. I have a master's degree in biblical studies, theology, and Christian education, and I also completed my doctorate in Christian education at the North Carolina College of Theology. My goal in furthering my education was to become more adept in healing and teaching.

I've been a member of the Beth-El Temple Church, which is also a satellite school for North Carolina College of Theology, for the last twenty-two years. There, I serve as vice president of the New Members Ministry. I teach new members to the ministry, the vision of the house and the heart of the leader. I'm in the Prayer Band, the Willing Workers, where we find a need and fill it for ministry, and the Family Enrichment Ministry, where we help members with writing and other skills needed in daily life.

I'm a nineteen-year employee of the Johns Hopkins Hospital in the radiology department, serving as a senior coordinator. When I'm not there, I'm working at Johns Hopkins Bayview in the triage department. In the nineteen years that I've worked on my job, I have never been late and I have never called out. Two years ago, I received the Edward Halle Award, which is the highest award you can receive at Johns Hopkins Hospital. It was during his tenure at Johns Hopkins that Edward Halle embodied the hospital's continued effort—to ensure patients had access to medical care and were treated with courtesy and respect. The award represents the institution's determination that employees should remember and emulate Halle's kindness.

The Edward Halle Award is earned by one person per year for caring for patients, demonstrating excellent customer service, and receiving commendations from patients who have taken the time to put their positive experience into words through the hospital's Service Excellence program. Service Excellence forms are located in boxes in each department. Patients fill them out and submit them through the boxes or by mail to the various department directors. The recipient is awarded five hundred dollars and a plaque. Now, the hospital has twenty-three thousand employees, so to be recognized by the institution is an even greater award than five hundred dollars. I have sown and planted so much; and because I have been so blessed, I know that I walk in God's favor. The list of His blessings is endless.

When I bought my house, the only thing I gave them was $14.66, and I believe that this was as a result of what I had sown. In other words, because I had sown financially and with my time and service, at church, on my job, and wherever I found a need, God blessed me. He made seemingly "impossible" things happen for me concerning my house. Sitting at the settlement table to purchase a house worth one hundred and sixty thousand dollars and only giving them $14.66 is not normal. It's favor. And this wasn't the only time that I've been blessed like that. For instance, I didn't even ask for the car I drive. I was not looking or praying for a new car.

I was praying for someone else—for several people actually—and in the midst of my prayer, God said, "Prepare for the blessing." I did as He instructed by beginning to thank Him in advance for whatever blessing was coming and preparing my heart and mind to expect the blessing. This was during my regular "after midnight" prayer time between Monday and Tuesday. After my prayer time, I looked through my mail, and I found one of those mailings that car dealerships periodically send out. Normally, I don't even read them, let alone call; however, this time, not even thinking about the lateness of the hour, I picked up my phone and dialed the number, not knowing that it was to a cell phone. My call went to voice mail, and I left a message saying that I was calling in response to the card I received in the mail. I left my number, and a salesman called me back.

The following day, I went to the car dealership because the salesman who called me asked me to meet with him. I wasn't looking for a car, but I was there for about an hour and drove off with a new car. In fact, my supervisor called me while I was there and asked if I could come and help them out because they were short in the ER. I said, "Sure, after I leave from the car place, I'll be right there." I had no clue that I'd be leaving with a new car. I gave them a hundred dollars down; I called my insurance company, and in less than five minutes, they had faxed every document the salesman needed. He said it was the fastest he had ever seen this happen. He had me meet with the business manager who said, "This is what I am going to do for you. There is just something special about you. I am not going to make your first payment due in thirty days. I am going to add fifteen more days so that your first payment will be due in forty-five days." On top of that, she bumped my payment down to $411.00 for a new Sonata. At that point, I'd had fourteen cars over the course of my life, but that was one of the lowest car payments I'd ever made.

I am constantly giving though, and I don't say that to brag (as I rarely ever tell people what I do for others) but to demonstrate the many opportunities that we have to give. Even when you think you don't have something to give, you do. And it doesn't always have to be money. Just the other day, for instance, I was in a cold parking lot. I took off a brand-new sweater to give to someone because it was cold, and the person was not adequately dressed for the weather. A lady asked, "Are you really going to do that for someone?" I said, "Yes, I am. I have more than enough. I am blessed to give the blessing." What is more important is that I was able to show someone that there are still good people who will help the less fortunate. I felt good about being able to do it. I knew that, as cold as it was, not many people would sacrifice their own comfort for someone else in this time in which we are living. They do not always remember the words of Jesus:

In as much as ye have done it unto one of the least of these my brethren, ye have done it unto Me.

Matthew 25:40

That was an expensive sweater that I gave away. Sometimes we give things away that we don't want, but what about the things that we *do* want? Are we willing to give that away to help somebody in a time of need?

We must always be careful of what and where we sow our seed, for every ground is not good ground. A farmer must toil the field and properly care for the field as he begins the process of planting seed for the harvest he expects to come. At some point in the process, he knows that what he plants and sows will grow into a harvest, but it all starts with a seed. The seed begins the process and becomes the power as it germinates underground. Just as it is in the natural, so it is in the spiritual. You must nurture and water your spirit while God gives the increase. As we plant seed, we can expect that the harvest will manifest in the God-appointed time and season. This is the biblical principle of "sowing and reaping." When you sow into "good ground," e.g., meeting the needs of others (including giving your time, possessions, and money, and doing whatever good you can wherever and whenever you have the opportunity), you will reap and receive God's favor in your life.

Agriculture involves knowing the process of the environment. We must know both the natural and spiritual power of the seed, and we can be assured of seedtime and harvest. As my former pastor, Apostle Evans, and my current pastor, Bishop Pender, taught me, when I seed into the kingdom, I should expect a harvest. However, when we deal with agriculture, timing and season mean everything. This is true spiritually as well. In other words, I have learned to give (sow seed) when the opportunity arises, and I have learned that I will reap (receive a harvest) that comes as God directs and in God's time). I have planted seed in the ground, and I'm always looking for my harvest to take place. In this season in my life, I am in great expectation of a bountiful harvest in all areas of my life. And it's not just financial or material gain. I am hoping for my family to be saved and delivered; I am looking for healing for my brothers and sisters. Blessedly, I've learned to give seed (plant and sow), and I thank God for allowing people in my life to teach me these great principals.

After the seedtime, the harvest will come at the appointed time. Sometimes we may sow; then, we reap. For example, I just got a raise at my job. And I not only got an increase at my job, I got an increase on a credit card debt. The credit card company said it was because I had met every payment and done it in advance. That wasn't something I was looking for at this time because I had been told that it wasn't to happen until much later. Often, people look for the financial part, however, reaping my harvest does not just mean in finances; it could be in healing. I am sowing to my healing, you know, the health of my body. There are times when someone is healed of cancer or some other disease about which you have prayed for healing. Perhaps you have prayed and sown a seed for your child who is sick, or that your child will finish college. It may be that I am sowing to my children's education down the line. Even though I don't have children now, what I have sown may ensure that they will be able to get an education when the time comes. Or my godchildren will be able to get the education that maybe their parents couldn't provide. Again, it's not only in the tangible—we can look for the harvest in the supernatural as well. Your sowing can also keep you and your loved ones from dangers, seen and unseen.

Just recently, in the emergency room at work, we had a victim of a shooting. He was only twenty-one years old. He was still living when I left, so somebody prayed along the way, somebody sowed along the way, somebody gave, and those seeds kept him alive. It could easily have gone another way. We have got to look further than just financial issues. Maybe you have a family member on drugs, and you determine that you are going to give, and you are going to sow, that they might be delivered. So in all these different ways, your planted seed produces something that you are expecting to one day come forth.

The power of the seed, once sown, has the ability and power to perform. The scripture says,

> *If ye have faith as a grain of mustard seed, ye*
> *shall say unto this mountain, Remove hence to*
> *yonder place; and it shall remove; and nothing*
> *shall be impossible unto you.*

Matthew 17:20

So you see, as tiny as the mustard seed is, it is powerful. The scripture illustrates the power of even a tiny seed that is planted and then watered by faith (the expectation that it will bring forth a harvest). It can become the voice of Christ. One of our choirs at the Beth-El Temple Church sings a song called "Mustard Seed Faith." Your seed and your faith will produce something very powerful, but you must believe, and you must plant. When one plants the seed in the ground, it's for a purpose and a reason. The seed can also affect your life naturally: for produce (food), a way of living (farming), agriculturally (a way of survival), and spiritually (sowing and looking for the harvest to manifest). Whatever seed you plant will grow and produce, so make sure you are sowing the right seed. If your sowing is not in alignment with God's Word, then you'll never reap the harvest that you're expecting.

When was the last time you planted and sowed seed?

How are you preparing for what's to come?

What are your expectations?

This book touches everyone in every stage, giving you enlightenment, encouragement, and hope. It will prompt you to go further. Another aspect of sowing brings us to the subject of tithing or giving to God the tenth of your income, through your church. Tithing is a biblical concept designed for the running and maintenance of the church and pastorate. For those of you who give the tithe in faith, you'll be reminded of what you have sown, what you have planted, and how you can look for the harvest that is to come. As you obey God in this area (tithing), you can be assured that blessings will follow because you are obeying God. The Word of God says,

Bring ye all the tithes into the storehouse, that there may be meat in mine house, and prove me now herewith, saith the Lord of hosts, if I will not open you the windows of heaven, and pour you out a blessing, that there shall not be room enough to receive it.

Malachi 3:10

His command to "prove me," is going to prompt God to do what he says He will do. He declares that He will open the windows of heaven and pour out a blessing that exceeds what we have given. But we have to remember that the principle is to "bring the tithes into the storehouse." Therefore, that is what we must do to receive the rest of His promise. We have to do it God's way in order to receive His promise.

My goal is to guide you in being more deliberate about what and where you plant and position you for the destination of the harvest.

PART I:

SOWING YOUR SEED

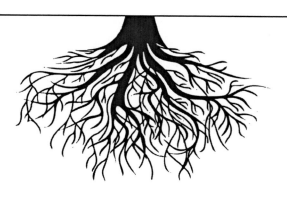

Everything points back to a seed—even Christ who was the ultimate seed. Webster's Dictionary defines seed as the fertilized egg of a plant, or the sperm of a male human or animal. As we observe life in general, there is evidence everywhere of seeds and sowing in the process. You and I started with a seed that had to be planted in an organ before it could grow.

Plants begin as seeds that are embedded in soil. When the seed is planted and the rain comes to water the earth, something will happen during that process. Each plant requires different environments and processes. We have no idea why certain plants grow only in one season, as compared to another, or why they bloom at certain times. Some plants are called annuals, meaning they live for one year, and others are called perennials, meaning the plant lives for more than two years. With annuals, you must buy the seeds and plant them every spring, but perennials will come back on their own each year.

BIBLICAL TESTAMENTS

Scripturally, or from a Hebrew point of view, seeds represent a person's descendants. This is evident as we look at the genealogies in Genesis, Matthew, Luke, and others.

Tracing the role of ancestry, the Bible points to Jesus as the Messiah through the seed of Abraham and relates to God's covenant promise to Abraham regarding his descendants.

In Ancient Israel, agriculture was an important part of the culture once the Israelites conquered Canaan and were no longer nomads living in tents. Seeding, sowing, and harvesting became familiar terms to the inhabitants. As an example, Ruth was sent to glean at harvest in the field of Boaz (Ruth 2:1–2). A bountiful harvest was seen as a blessing. Jesus taught in parables, and prominent parables compared the role of sowing and seeding to life's problems, pressures, and successes. The individuals to whom Jesus spoke these things understood that you sow or plant with the expectation of a harvest. It would have been clear to them that you cannot reap a harvest if you don't sow properly.

Matthew 25:14–30 relates one of the parables with which Jesus taught His disciples. He told them of a presumably wealthy man who called in three of his servants before he left to travel and gave each of them talents according to their abilities. A talent was about $1,000 in silver content. One servant was given five talents, another was given two talents, and the third servant was given one talent. The man who was given five talents invested them and made an additional five talents. The man who was given two talents, likewise, doubled what he had been given. However, the man who was given only one talent hid it in the ground. He did not follow the sowing principle (i.e., sow or plant what you have wisely, so that it will prosper and grow). Instead of sowing or planting (investing wisely) the talent, he buried (hid) it in the ground. In other words, he didn't "plant" it so that it could grow, he tucked it away, and therefore, had no increase.

When the master returned, the third servant was punished because he did not try to increase what he had been given. Consequently, he lost even that. God wants us to sow what we have into good ground. That is the only way that we realize a harvest. Your "seed" can include your time, your finances, or your abilities. Good ground is that person, place, area, project, etc., that offers a good return. If we simply hold on to our seed, whatever it might be, we limit that seed's ability to grow. We can't just take something, hide it (do nothing to improve upon it), and expect something to grow from it. Like a closed hand that neither releases nor receives anything, an uninvested (unsowed/unplanted) seed will never produce a harvest.

The master (who represents God) expected his servants to go out and do something with what he gave them. The servants with the two and the five talents produced more of what was originally given to them. This demonstrated to the master that they could be trusted with even greater things, and he rewarded them thusly. A lot of times we don't just get blessed by blessing ourselves. We have to bless someone else in order for blessings to come to us.

In the Synoptic Gospels of Matthew (13:3–8), Mark (4:3–8) and Luke (8:5–15), the parable of the sower and the seed is presented. It describes the Kingdom of Heaven as likened to a sower who went forth to sow seeds. This process involved the farmer carrying seed in a leather pouch on his shoulder. He took the seeds from the pouch, and with a practiced movement, scattered them evenly on the ground. The parable illustrates how the seed arrived on the ground, the type of ground the seed fell on, and the effect of that type of ground on the life and growth of the seed.

*And he spake many things unto them in parables,
saying, Behold, a sower went forth to sow;*

*And when he sowed, some seeds fell by the way
side, and the fowls came and devoured them up:*

*Some fell upon stony places, where they had
not much earth: and forthwith they sprung up,
because they had no deepness of earth:*

*And when the sun was up, they were scorched;
and because they had no root, they withered
away.*

*And some fell among thorns; and the thorns
sprung up, and choked them:*

*But other fell into good ground, and brought
forth fruit, some an hundredfold, some sixtyfold,
some thirtyfold.*

Matthew 13:3–8:3

Both Mark and Luke similarly record this parable.

Jesus identifies the field or ground as the world and the seed as God's Word. The sower represents the one who delivers the Word of God to the world (preacher, teacher, etc.). The types of ground illustrate the levels of maturity of the hearers and their reactions to God's Word. In Matthew 13:18–23, Jesus further explains the Parable of the Sower by clearly describing what happens when the seed falls on the various types of ground:

Hear ye therefore the parable of the sower.

When any one heareth the word of the kingdom, and understandeth it not, then cometh the wicked one, and catcheth away that which was sown in his heart. This is he which received seed by the way side.

But he that received the seed into stony places, the same is he that heareth the word, and anon with joy receiveth it;

Yet hath he not root in himself, but dureth for a while: for when tribulation or persecution ariseth because of the word, by and by he is offended.

He also that received seed among the thorns is he that heareth the word; and the care of this world, and the deceitfulness of riches, choke the word, and he becometh unfruitful.

But he that received seed into the good ground is he that heareth the word, and understandeth it; which also beareth fruit, and bringeth forth, some an hundredfold, some sixty, some thirty.

The seed that falls on the good ground represents those persons who hear the Word of God, and, receiving it in their hearts, go forth to live according to the Word and spread the Word to as many others as possible. This parable describes the present-day world and people's reactions upon hearing God's Word.

The Parable of the Wheat and Tares also describes what the Kingdom of Heaven is like. A man sowed good seed in his field and goes to sleep, only to have the enemy come and sow tares among the wheat. Tares are defined as weeds, and they resemble wheat in early stages of growth. They can trick us if we're not careful. As tares grow, they cease resembling wheat, but their roots are already interwoven with the wheat. You cannot destroy the tares without endangering the real wheat plants, which is why they are told to grow them together until harvest time.

In John 12:24, Jesus compares his death to a seed that died once it was planted in the ground, but renewed itself through the plant it generated. The gospel states,

Verily, verily, I say unto you, Except a corn of wheat fall into the ground and die, it abideth alone: but if it die, it bringeth forth much fruit.

When you seed into the ground, you have to sow into the right ground and the right soil, so the condition of the ground doesn't choke the seed. If you have weeds around the seed, they may hinder the growth of the seed.

Consider your yard—let's say you're planting new grass. If you don't clear the weeds, they may choke the growth of what you have planted. The weeds must be pulled up. Even in our lives, some things have to be uprooted for new growth to take place. You can't do something different with the same point of view. You can't be in one place trying to get to another if you have not dealt with any unresolved issues in the place you want to leave. This illustrates the roles of the world being intertwined: God and Satan, believers and non-believers. Today, we as believers must emphasize the role of the Kingdom in terms of planting and reaping.

HEAR, MODEL, AND TEACH GOD'S WORD

Paul asks the question in Romans 10:14 (b): "How shall they hear without a preacher?" Paul tells us that we must hear the Word of God in order for us to believe it. Then, we have to apply the Word. The Bible says that we are not to be just hearers of the Word, but we must be doers of the Word, also. We have to be the example of what God says in His Word. We have to be the model of what He has taught, all He has given, His commandments, and His principles. I can't say that I believe and practice the Ten

Commandments (e.g., thou shalt not steal or kill), if I go out and do those things. And as we go out and apply that which is in us to help somebody else, we must model what we believe. Your life is an example that others may see and desire to come into the church.

Here is a prime example: I prayed for a paramedic one day. She sat with a whole group in the emergency room when she dropped off her patient. She had been experiencing difficulty with adopting a child who had been with her for a very long time. It was time to go to court and the grandparents had taken the child out of State. Even though this young lady had provided all of the paperwork and other documentation that the court required, she was afraid that she would lose custody of the child. She said, "I listen to the prayer line that you do because I started having anxiety attacks, and it has encouraged me." After praying with her, I told her that, in this situation, she was doing everything that she should and everything in alignment with the court's instructions. I said, "You cannot allow anyone to distract you or take you off course. The enemy comes in when you get distracted, and that is why you began having these panic attacks. You start thinking that the promise that God has already made to you is going to be null and void." I also told her that she had to depend on what she knew. In other words, she had done everything she was supposed to do. She had a receipt from the court indicating that she had submitted the appropriate documentation, so everything was working for her. I said, "I served on the grand jury for four months, and I saw firsthand that having pertinent documentation and evidence will take you a long way in court." Our talk and her persistence in listening to the prayer line caused her to look at her situation in another way.

Somebody may never walk into a church or know which direction to take, but if they see you, your integrity and your character will speak volumes. Somebody is always watching, so we must apply what we know from God's Word to every situation. We have to live and reflect what God says because we don't know the next person that we may affect. We may have the word that could cause somebody to live, have hope, and not give up. My buddy, Randy Roberts, said I would always encourage him when I would say, "Don't give up. We can't give up on our dreams. If God has given us a dream, we have got to look for the manifestation but keep dreaming. It is only when we stop dreaming that the dream doesn't become a reality. Consider the publishing company that I went through to write this book. What if the owner would have stopped dreaming? You might not be reading this today.

I wasn't always the dedicated believer that I am now. I was eighteen when I rededicated my life to Christ. It was on my mother's birthday, October 12, 1986, at my mother's church. I was raised in the church because I had to go, but my heart wasn't in it like it was when I decided to recommit on my own. We didn't have all of the options that these twenty-first century children enjoy. For instance, now, if children don't want to go to church on a particular Sunday, they are allowed to stay at home. When I was growing up, everybody in the house went to church on Sunday. That was the rule, and in those days, you followed the rules and that was that. Going to church was a part of our heritage, but church attendance did not give me a relationship with God. I couldn't get by on my mother's relationship. I needed to develop my own relationship with God, and nobody could do that but me.

I used to like to party. I was among the "who's who" of the best dancers when I was in high school, and I am acknowledged as such in the yearbook because I loved to dance. Nowadays, I still dance a lot, but it is in church. I love to, you know, have celebrations, so even when people look at me now, they respect me because I have never judged others based on their situations or their circumstances. People respect me to the highest because even though they may not be where I am, we all have a process to go through, and they know that I try to see them as God sees them. I allude to this on the prayer line. You can't look at where people are right now; you have to look a little bit further to see where they may be going. I try not to judge some of the people I know who may not be saved or may not be in the church.

I once had a conversation with a gentleman who had just joined the church. He said, "You know, Eric, I have not been completely delivered from cigarettes; I still smoke." I said to him, "We all have something that we are dealing with, and it's not an overnight process. But God looks at the sincerity of your heart. Be truthful and honest because God can work with you when you are honestly trying to be and do better, and He will help you." I repeated to him 1 Samuel 16:7(b):

For the Lord seeth not as man seeth; for man looketh on the outward appearance, but the Lord looketh on the heart.

The outward appearance may look wonderful but what does my inside say? What does my heart say? What do my actions say? That makes a difference. And I gained the trust of this person. He ended up calling me one day because he had to go the emergency room. He was having trouble getting his prescriptions, so I helped him by referring him to a friend who worked there. When he called to thank me, he also asked me if I could get him a Bible. I told him that I absolutely would get one for him, and I brought the Bible to him on the following Sunday. It made a world of difference in his life. My word is my bond. Integrity and character will take you a long way in life, and that's what people are going to remember.

Everyone has a gift, whatever their function, whatever their purpose. I may be a teacher, but you may be a singer. There are people who teach professionally, e.g., schoolteachers, but they don't teach spiritual matters.

You may know someone who is a writer, or another person may love to talk it out but have someone else write it. In our lives, we are all called to minister because it is just that—*our* lives. We can always help somebody, or somebody can always help us. I always wanted to teach in front of people, but I didn't have the confidence to do so. However, I taught a lesson in our Bible college where all of the classes—the associates, the bachelors, the masters, the doctorates—came together to hear me speak. It was so phenomenal because so many people, even the older ones, said, "You broke it down to our understanding." I was in awe. I told somebody that I knew I wanted to teach, but it needed to be pulled out of me. Not everyone can be a teacher, but you *can* tell people your life story, through your gift and your testimony.

You can go to a job not knowing all of the duties, but you can be taught how to perform them. However, in spite of you learning the job, it may not be right for you. When people come out of college, for instance, they may go into their professions. They have the basic ability to do the job, but they have to learn the craft, and they have to learn the position. They have to learn from somebody who has the wisdom and the knowledge and who has already mastered the job that the new recruits are trying to learn. On the other side, when we are the ones with the experience, wisdom, and knowledge, we need to be willing to help someone out.

WORSHIP IN GIVING

Giving is a part of worship. As you sow in church and give seed, it's amazing how you will be blessed, expectedly and unexpectedly. Your seed has the power to release God's harvest; your seed has the power and ability to cause healing and prosperity. The Bible says,

> *He which soweth sparingly shall reap also sparingly; and he which soweth bountifully shall reap also bountifully.*

2 Corinthians 9:6

God loves a cheerful giver. My brothers and sisters, I challenge you to sow, give, and tithe. When you do, do it with the right heart, the right motive, the right attitude.

You can expect God to honor His Word. Watch God move on your behalf. In John 15:7, He says,

> *If you abide in Me, and My words abide in you,*
> *ye shall ask what ye will, and it shall*
> *be done unto you.*

So I ask because I am abiding in Him, and He in me, so, I expect God to honor His Word. I have to do my part so He can do His.

In the Bible, Paul recognizes God as the great supplier—whatever we have to give was first given to us by God. Paul was, as we know, one of the great apostles. Paul also wrote two thirds of the New Testament, and what was so interesting is that he was converted from Saul to Paul. God shifted his whole life to be a great ambassador for Him, and he wrote most of the New Testament from prison. So when you have been called and been chosen, it doesn't matter where you started, it is how you finish. It is not how fast you run but that you endure. When there is purpose on your life and when there is purpose and destiny in the journey to where you are going, it is important that you keep on moving.

Look at the story of the turtle and the hare—the key wasn't how fast the turtle was going, it was that he kept on going. He endured and finished the race. The rabbit laughed and took a break. Sometimes, if you look at other people's process instead of focusing on your own, you may stop, but if you keep going, you are going to cross the finish line first. Paul continued on his journey no matter what. He kept on writing, and even in prison, his letters reached the various New Testament churches with necessary instructions and encouragement. And the messages in those letters are still relevant for us today because we are still blessed by what God inspired in him. All these years later, we are still benefiting from what was implanted in Paul. We benefit from the results of generous giving. You will reap what you sow when you sow in good ground, and you will produce a harvest.

EQUATE YOUR NAME WITH EXCELLENCE

My mother always taught us to be the best that we can be. We know that no one is perfect but God. We strive for perfection and to perfect the things that we do, whether it be in our careers, our trades, or our crafts. In anything that we are trying to perfect, we have to continue to work at it. I strive for excellence because it speaks of my character and my demeanor; it speaks of who I am, so I always want to strive to do my best and be my best.

When we give our best, others might look at us and think, "Well, how did you get to this place?" With perseverance, endurance, and striving to be the best that I can be, taking every avenue that would help me to be a better me. For example, I take a lot of classes at work, especially those classes that deal with improving patient relations and care and methods for improving how we work. In my review, my manager said, "Wow, Eric, you really take a lot of classes," and I said to her, "Not only does it help me, but it helps the clinic and the area in which I work." It is allotted to me as a benefit for working for the institution, so I take advantage of all of that. It makes sense to me to make full use of it. I also read up on people who've been excelling and how they got to where they are. It helps me to understand and improve my job performance. I try to follow some of the wisdom and knowledge displayed by others who have excelled. As somebody who already has reached the place that I am trying to go, these successful others have some of the wisdom and knowledge to help me get where I need to go.

Everybody's circumstances and situations are different. People may look to see that I have achieved success in a numbers of areas of endeavor, and I count it a privilege and honor to be in that position. I know I am blessed. I have also seen how my mother went to work every day and how she was such a hard worker to provide and take care of all eight of us. Granted, not everybody has the same drive to push through in order to get to work in difficult times—like during a recent blizzard. Some people just could not make it in. Since my car was buried in the snow, and I wasn't able to get it out, I took a step further to see if there was another way to get to work. What I did was this: I called around and reached my clinic manager who drives a truck, and he was willing to come pick me up so that I could get in to work to help do the job in my area. I might not have succeeded in getting to work if I hadn't pursued a ride.

About ten years ago, there was a command center in the ER at Bayview that provided rides for employees during inclement weather conditions. All you had to do was call in to the command center. You requested pick up, then provided pertinent information about your home location, where you worked, and if you could get to the nearest major cross street. I did what I needed to do to get to my job. I even packed an overnight bag and stayed a couple of days during a bad snowstorm. I relate this to show that we must look for opportunities to take the initiative to get things done. Look for help for your situation before you give up; it shows you in a positive light to employers and fellow employees. So in this instance, I made the extra call. I found out who lived close by me and was willing to pick me up, and I was ready and on my porch when they came.

It took a lot of work to get to the point where I am now; I am always working hard at it. Like anything else, as I mentioned before, no one is perfect. However, you strive to be better; you strive for perfection in all that you do. Certainly, there have been many challenges during the nineteen years that I have worked at Hopkins, but I always try to persevere. I ask myself, "What can I do better? What can I learn from every experience in which I find myself?"

Sixteen years ago, I was blamed for something that I didn't do. The individual who *was* to blame never spoke up and admitted it. When other people learned of the situation, they wrote letters and came to my defense. I learned something from this situation. I learned not to be bitter and not to blame anyone, but to continue to strive and do my best. When those who were involved then see me now, they can't ever say that I blamed them or displayed any bitterness. It only made me better.

God requires excellence from us—not just settling for the basics, but going above and beyond is a part of the process of sowing and reaping. If you sow in greatness, then you expect to reap greatness as well. He wants us to excel in character: who we are and what we do. Everything you do should be to the glory of God. That said, the ultimate goal in giving, whether on the job, in your marriage, in your relationship with your children, in tithing, in volunteering your time, etc., is to pursue excellence. Doing so is also an indication of spiritual maturity.

In Proverbs 22:1, the Bible says that a good name is preferred to great riches. This means that I should want my name to be great, and that is what God desires for each of us. His is the ultimate great name, and we are to model Him before the world. When people mention my name or people see me, what would they really say if they think about Eric? What would the conversation be? I want my name to stand for something positive. Not that I don't want great riches too, but I would rather have my integrity and my good character because they will take me a long way in life. I always want to be found trying to be excellent in doing all I can and being all I can so that God might be pleased with my life. Because, at the conclusion of it all, I do want to hear Him say, "Well done." I don't want people to find it difficult to think of good things to say about me at my funeral, for instance.

What would my life say? Have I lived my life well in spite of the good, the bad, and the indifferent that may have occurred? Has my life touched somebody else's life? Have I encouraged someone? Has someone looked at me as an example? What would my name say when it is all said and done? I would want to know that others patterned themselves after me and strived to do the things I did. I want to leave a legacy. I want to leave a mark. I don't want people to have to reach for something good to say. I want them to think, "Oh wow, he has touched my life. He has encouraged someone. He has helped someone who was less fortunate. He has fed somebody that was hungry." When I have done that, I will have done it as unto my God.

EXPECT A HARVEST

You can expect a harvest because the Word said to "be not weary in well doing" (2 Thessalonians 3:13). So even then, He gave us a pattern of behavior to follow. We have something coming because of what we did and the part that we played. In Isaiah 55, God says His Word is not going to return to Him void. He gives us instruction. He gives direction, but then He reveals what will come out of what we have done. I can expect something to come out of what I have seeded and planted because my mindset is if I seed and plant, or even if I give, it shall be given back to me: "good measure, pressed down, shaken together and running over" (Luke 6:38). So when I give, I have the expectation that there is something to come afterwards. I am in great expectation of the harvest my seed will produce from what I planted. The scripture says he who soweth in abundance shall reap in abundance. When we continue to sow seed, it will produce a harvest.

When one plants the seed in the ground, it's for a purpose and a reason. I learned to attach a prayer to my seed and name what I needed my seed to do and where I needed my seed to go. As I put a seed offering in my envelope, I write where I need to apply it and where I need it to go, for example, for my family or for becoming debt-free. I sow to it, and as it happens, I check it off my list. I do this every time I tithe, give my seed offering, or even if I give sacrificially. I have a list that I wrote seven things on, and as each thing happens, I tick it off knowing that that was something that was done based on the seed I planted. It may happen tomorrow, it may happen down the road, it may happen in a mall. Every day, I am in expectation for it to happen. I still look in my mailbox every day for unexpected blessings. Once I check something off, I start all over again and have another expectation. So it's a continuation that we just don't stop. I am dreaming. I have to keep on dreaming.

Just because one thing happens, why stop dreaming when there can be something else that I am looking for? I wrote it down so I know it's prayed over, and sometimes I need a memory of what I did. So when I write it and my mind goes back to when it happens, I look and say I wrote that down. Sometimes you have to believe it before you see it and write it down so you can recognize it when it comes. So in my writing, sometimes I go back to when God has told me something specific in prayer. God referenced something that He had told me previously when he said to me in prayer, "Go back and revisit the dreams and the promises." They are still good. A long time ago, I wrote something down in reference to a vision for a clothing line. I went back and pulled it out. I reread what I wrote, and now I am reminded of the expectation. Words are powerful.

While I was working for the institution of JHH, I spoke with a coworker who had been there for forty-nine years and was retiring. I asked her, "What kept you here? I have seen you every day; you have endured many circumstances and situations. What was it that kept you this long?" I told her about the power of the seed and the name of this book, and she said that she, too, has sown. She began to tell me how she endured and was able to stay at the institution for so many years and how she overcame many obstacles and even how she sowed into the lives of others. She always tried to do the right thing, to do her job well, and to treat others as she wanted to be treated. This was so even when she was *not* treated well. As she went, she helped others along the way, and those seeds provided for her a harvest of longevity. I further understood then how powerful the seed can be.

You can be in difficult circumstances now, but later you are going to reap what you have sown. For some who have longevity, there has to be some wisdom, some knowledge, some tenacity, and some endurance. There have to be some circumstances and situations to overcome, but the conclusion is, they made it. What have you endured? And how can you pour that into somebody else to help them to know that they can still make it?

PART II :

NURTURING YOUR SEED

Once the seed is planted, it begins an underground process to develop and eventually manifest. While the seed is underground, your job is to nurture it. One must continue to till the field, water the seed, and overturn the dirt to continue the germination of the soil, so the seed may continue its process of sprouting. Your seed will also require the elements of water, sun, and the appropriate climate in order to grow. If you just plant it and there is no nurturing of it, then nothing will become of it; it will die. If you've ever kept plants, then you know that you have to keep an eye on them. Whenever leaves begin turning brown, you have to take those off for the green to continue to grow. You have to remove the weeds around it. You have to water it and make sure that it's getting adequate sunlight. And if it outgrows its pot, then you have to replant it in another.

Farmers save some of their crops for food and sell the rest. Then, the process starts all over again. Agriculture is the farmer's means of life and survival. If he stops planting and nurturing, if he stops germinating, if he stops fueling the process, he has cut off the harvest and his supply. If I don't continue my process of what I know to be true and right, even with working, planning, sowing, and nurturing the entire process, how can I expect to go to another level? How can I look for something to come if I stop a process that I know works?

Learning to nurture your seed is a generational benefit. The more you do it, the better chance you'll have of something greater coming to your children, grandchildren, great-grandchildren, and other loved ones—and it doesn't have to be biological. I've sown seeds by helping people on the job, in the community, and at the church. I have the best neighbors and was blessed to watch one of their children grow and go to college. As often as I can, I invest seeds so that young people will have what they need and want as they go through college. I believe in the sowing and reaping principle, and if I invest now, I will reap the dividend later. I always want to be a blessing to others.

If we continue to help the upcoming generation get to where they need to go, we are investing in a future. I am also sowing for several young people in my church who are in their first year of college. I am investing in their college to ensure that I can take a part in helping them finish. I was so proud to know that each of them brought home straight As because I knew I was investing in something good. It is important that they finish, that they make it, that they become successful, that they become a productive member of society, that they go through school and further their education—that they don't have to give up or fail like some of us may have done. We don't want them to stop and say, "Oh I can't finish this, I can't make it." Instead, our help and support says, "You can make it and you can finish, because here, I am going to help you. I am going to invest in you. I am going to do my part to make sure you succeed."

Later on, we can see the dividend when they walk across the stage to graduate, or when they get that invitation in the mail that says they are candidates for a bachelor's degree or a master's program—all because somebody invested in them. They can say, "I may have had some struggles along the way, but I still made it. I may have had some situations along the way, but I made it. I may have needed a tutor, but I made it." So the investment that we make in them produces something greater, and we can say that we played a part.

DR. ERIC L. HOLMES

BE PATIENT

Oftentimes, we go through a process but never want to experience it fully. You cannot rush the process or the manifestation. Years ago, Apostle Evans said, "I never want a blessing prematurely because I may not be able to handle it." This statement is powerful and still stands true today. We want things, but we want them on our own time. We never want to go through what it takes to get these things because we're in a "microwave" age, meaning we want everything fast.

God can do things suddenly if he chooses, but He doesn't need our help. He knows all about our process and knows that His appointed time is for our own good. As we continue the process of the power of the seed, we understand that it must fully evolve in order for us to see the greatest results of what has been sown. The harvest will come at a set time. If I wait on God, I know the manifestation of what I have sown, planted, and seeded will come to fullness in the right time.

One day, I was asked to do an opening prayer at the album release for Randy Roberts, who used to sing for the boys' choir. Before I began praying, he said, "I waited

60

three years for the album release, and along the way, Dr. E encouraged me not to give up, because at the appointed time, it would happen." That one conversation that we had in the elevator and those seeds that I'd drop in his ear here and there added up. He waited until the right season to release the project he had worked on in order for it to be effective. And it was very successful because it wasn't rushed.

BE NOT WEARY

Sometimes we get a little weary along the way. We want it to happen on January 7, but the right time might be the following November 20. Trusting the process is going to be worth it in the end. Be careful not to treat your dream like a meal at a fast-food counter. Sometimes things have to be slow-cooked. A diamond, for example, has to undergo intense heat and pressure to become the beloved jewel that we know it to be. Gold must be sent through the fire to remove any of its impurities. If you take it out before it's finished, you won't have the precious metal because it won't be fully processed. Likewise, the seed must germinate for it to be fully processed in order for the harvest to be full. It may be the following year, it may be two years, or it may be ten years, but the set time that it has is going to determine how full the harvest is.

The power of the seed will bring things you cannot imagine. Remember, he who soweth in abundance shall reap in abundance (2 Corinthians 9:6). Whenever you are going through the process, you are going to feel the heat, you are going to feel the discomfort, and you'll wonder why you're going through all of it. Take a moment to step outside of your circumstances and observe. Pain produces purpose to get you through your process and to get you to your destiny. But you have to feel something.

Jesus was in pain, even in the garden when He said, "Let this cup pass from me" (Matthew 26:39). He was uncomfortable. He could have gone another way, but then where would we be? Hard as it may have been, He was on the right road. The process that we have to go through—just like with the diamond or even the pearl (you have to go to the bottom of the ocean to find the pearl)—can't be rushed in order for it to be what it needs to be. If you never go to the bottom of the ocean, you never get the pearl.

Some circumstances will require you to look at them from another perspective. There have been moments when I've had to remind myself to go back to the basics. Go back to what I know. Go back to what was spoken in order to keep me looking and focused in the right direction, no matter how the winds may blow. Galatians 6:9 prompts us to "be not weary in well doing: for in due season we shall reap, if we faint not." Hold on until you see the manifestation of the seed or seeds you have planted.

No matter what the situation is, stay focused and don't mind the interruptions; don't mind how it's going. Know that you have something coming. If you are in expectation, no matter what month your birthday is in, you know you have got something coming. Children wait all year for Christmas because they know that on December 25, their presents are coming. Psalms 46:10 says, "Be still and know." Your promise is in transition, along with the answer.

GET INTO POSITION

Sometimes you have to prepare for what's to come even when you don't know when it's coming. When preparing for my house, I began moving things out and getting into posture for what was to come. One of the young ladies on my job shared with me that her daughter was moving into her first apartment, and God laid it on my heart to give her one of my practically new bedroom sets. I had another set that was valued at almost $2,500 and gave it to my nephew, not knowing that he had just moved into a place with no furniture. When it came time to purchase my furniture, I found a deal that dropped the price and gave me more furniture than I started with.

I am ready, and I am preparing for what's to come because I have positioned myself. I have gotten in the posture to receive because I have sown so much, I have given so much, and I have planted so much. I still refer to the scripture that says there is seedtime and harvest, and I don't have to get weary because my harvest time is here since I have sown and I have planted. I look for a raise in my job because I am a good employee. I come to work and I give them good service. We are entitled to yearly evaluations, and sometimes they look back and give you a greater pay increase. To get a 5 percent increase at Johns Hopkins is hard to do. Not only does it have to go through the COO, but it has to be approved and signed off by supervisors, department heads, etc., and they want to know why this employee deserves it. Well, my vice chair looked back at my record and saw that I was a good employee and had been coming to work without ever coming in late or calling in sick. Without hesitation, she signed off on my increase, and I got that raise *plus* my yearly increase.

Get in the right position and in the right mindset. Always look at the positive and continue seeding and giving, and expect to reap a harvest. Martin Luther King Jr. defined faith as taking the first step even when you don't see the whole staircase. It may seem that nothing is moving in the direction that you want it to, but make room for it anyway. Get into the posture to receive by preparing for what's to come. Rejoice always, and again I say, rejoice, even when it looks like you are not receiving a harvest, or your harvest may be held up. Sometimes you have to look beyond what you see, because when it does happen, you can recognize it. You have to look further than what you presently see, because if you look at your present situation, it seems to dictate something else. *You have to look beyond.* If I am standing here and seeing the finish line there, I know that at some point I have to get there, but I will never get there if I am looking at where I am standing. I have to see myself at that finish line.

"He that goeth forth and weepeth, bearing precious seed, shall doubtless come again with rejoicing, bringing his sheaves with him."

(Psalm 126:6)

KNOW WHO YOU ARE

Know who you are and know whose you are as well. No matter what the odds are against you, you still can be successful. I even use that at my job. Regardless of what others may have thought, I knew what was in me and what others saw caused me to give. The year I received the Edward Halle Award because of the patience and care that I give to customer service, it turned out that I also received recognition from the mayor's office—all of that in one year. The COO said, "I'm so honored to present this to you. I have never, in all my thirty years here, seen anyone get the Martin Luther King Award and turn around and get the Edward Halle Award."

You have to know when the odds are against you—keep doing what you do and keep focusing on the positive, not the negative. Dare to be different, but know that it will cost you to shine above. I can remember these words from Apostle Evans, and I will keep using them because they impacted my life: "If you do what others won't do, you will be able to do what they can't do." That keeps me going and keeps me focused. From the harvest that is produced, you may see positive changes in finances, family, health, peace, and so many other things that will reveal the value and purpose of the discomfort.

One of the greatest lessons of discomfort is Mary carrying Jesus. Though she was carrying the most precious seed anyone could ever carry, she was ridiculed and shamed. During your seeding process, you may be talked about, too. You may feel that you're not going in the right direction, but look again. We have to look at it through the eyes of faith. Look at it through the eyes of grace and say this is producing for me a far greater purpose than where I am right now. At a sermon over fifteen years ago, I heard, "Don't look at what you presently see. You've got to look to what it can become." Because if you look at it from the natural light now, you will never move to the next dimension or level of where you need to go.

Don't allow the opinions of others to obstruct what

God told you is yours. People may have counted you out, but do you know what's in you? Do you know who you are?

I haven't always been in the position that I am now—to be able to give as lavishly as I do and receive such high rewards. Many times in my life, I was the one in need. And someone was always there to lend a helping hand. I have always been the spoiled one. There were eight of us, and I was number seven. My brothers and sisters all spoiled me. They have always taken care of me. And even when I moved and joined the Bethel Temple Church, the late Apostle Robert Evans became like a father to me and poured so much into my life.

One time, I had this really bad sinus infection close to my brain, and I didn't even know, so I went to work. My friend said to me, "You gotta go to the ER. You can't sit at this desk and work." I went to the ER, and they did a CAT scan and all of that. I didn't know what was going on, and when you don't know what's going on, you worry. When I was seven weeks old, I had an operation where the doctors told my mother that I wasn't going to live. At the time of this sinus infection, I was forty-eight, but the trauma brought back what I had been told about the time when I was seven weeks old and couldn't hold anything down.

My mother said that you could actually see inside my head. I was very sick. I have a scar on my stomach and on my arm and leg where they had to operate, but when they opened me up, they could not find anything wrong. That's why I can tell people, "I know He is a healer."

Even through the transitions of life that I have had to face, I have been blessed to have help. My sister, who now is sixty-four, helped me. She still helps me today. I mean, for a while, she paid for everything for me, along with my mom. Before I started working at Hopkins, I moved to Baltimore and worked in a temp job. Man, I was calling my sister like, "Big Sis, you know your brother needs some help." Even if I didn't say anything, because we are so close and connected, all eight of us, my sister always knew there was something I needed or she would call me.

She helped me so much, and that's why I try to help others. I know what it is to have my mortgage or my car note due and have no money to pay them. I have had a car repossessed, and it was not just because of mismanaged money. Once, our entire payroll was messed up, but the car company didn't want to hear anything about that, so I can tell people I know what it is to be without money.

When I moved from my apartment to my town house, and I was working all these hours, I made a vow to God. I vowed, "God, whatever you do, help me to be a good steward over my money." Before this vow, whatever I wanted, I bought. You can't live like that for long unless you were born really rich. My sister said to me, "Get a brown bag, and whatever it is, whether one dollar or two dollars, put it in there, because if an emergency arises, you will be able to take care of it." All of the wisdom and concepts that people have poured into my life have helped me. These ideas about saving, even small amounts, and living within my means helped me to get to where I am today—not only being a good steward with my money but being able to seed into others' lives.

The Word talks about being a good steward over what God has given us. My present pastor, Bishop Pender, teaches money management. He is phenomenal. He was the director of finance for many years at a Ford Motor dealership, and he helps me understand how to manage money and how to be a good steward. So when I had to put in a new furnace, hot water tank, sump pump, and washing machine, I was able to pay for every single thing. I have learned that to be a good manager, you don't spend everything you get. If you spend everything you get, then what are you going to do? You might not be able to call on your brother or sister (though these family members have helped me along the way). I've been lucky. I help others when I can because it's the rule of reciprocity (i.e., what you give out freely will come back to you). When you are open-handed with your blessings to others, God will bless you. That's why I can talk about the power of the seed. That's why I can talk about when and what you sow. It may not be today, and it may not be tomorrow, but somewhere down the road, you will reap what you have sown.

Favor is better than money in the bank.

Let me tell you about favor and your integrity and credibility. I recently had my account hacked, so I went to the bank to get the situation handled. One company kept adding charges to my account, and that really messed up everything because I had checks coming in. One of the checks was to my college. I wrote the check knowing that I had the money. The VP of the bank and the staff were phenomenally helpful. First of all, they emailed everything so I didn't have to go in there. But when I eventually did have to go in there to sign the affidavit, the VP said, "Eric, this is what I am going to do." They credited every single thing back to me. They moved one account to another and shut the other one down. I was at the bank for almost two hours.

My check to the college and every check that I'd written were covered. Of course, I contacted those to whom I'd written checks, as necessary. And because the bank helped to clear up the problem, my integrity was not questioned. They were so glad that I sat down with them, and it made me feel good, because there was a time when I had an overdraft. There is no way that I would just write a check trying to beat the bank. You can't do that now because electronic transactions are too fast. So I can tell people about the experience of having a car repossessed and about getting yellow eviction notices that apartment services posted on the outside of my door so that the whole apartment complex could see it. I can talk about having temp services cut your hours, knowing that you got one of those slips. But you know what it taught me, the process of it all? Always stay ahead. Now, I make my mortgage payments as early as possible—before they are due—and I usually have another payment in readiness for the following month's due date before it comes.

Always stay ahead, but always manage to be a good

steward over what you have. There is an old gospel song that says, "If I can help somebody along the way, then my living will not be in vain." That's why I am always trying to help somebody else. I know I have to help somebody along this way, and if I keep on living, *I* am going to need help again. Helping somebody might mean in finances, wisdom, a need for some specific knowledge, or it might be something small like helping a neighbor put together furniture. The little things matter, so I take nothing for granted. I can tell you the outcome of sowing: if you follow the principle in God's Word, you will reap and receive back what you have given out—often with an increase. As long as you plant, as long as you sow, something's got to come up later.

PART III:

HARVESTING YOUR SEED

One Saturday morning, I opened the door to the deck after my regular prayer time and looked at the tree in my backyard. It had been over ten years since I saw that tree bloom, and I really had never looked at the tree again until that morning. The Lord told me to take another look. "Look at it from another perspective," He said. When I looked at it again, it had pink and white flowers all over it; it was beautiful. He said then, "Your season has changed." What surprised me was that in nine years, I had never looked at the tree like that until God said to take another look. My harvest was there, and I just hadn't seen it. All I could say was, "My seed has gone from a seed to a tree, but it pointed back to the seed." That's actually where I got the title of this book, *The Power of the Seed*.

A harvest is the gathering of a crop; the time of gathering; the outcome of any action. We're in a harvest season now. Yes, we are in our due season and in this season, be careful not to miss your harvest for your tears. You may have cried a lot of tears, and your tears have been your "meat and drink" day and night, but joy does come in the morning. Something good is coming out of all the tears you cried. Just don't miss it by becoming focused on the tears you had to cry.

Weeping may endure for a night,
but joy cometh in the morning.

Psalm 30:5

Those that sow in tears shall reap in joy.

Psalm 126:5

Sometimes we miss what we have because we have cried so much. We have allowed our circumstance or our situation to dictate our future. We may have gotten so overwhelmed that we can't see further than where we are. We may cry so much that our eyes become so watery and unfocused that we can't see that there is something more in store for us.

As the psalm mentioned above tells us, joy comes in the morning. When you consider it, if your weeping endures for a night and joy comes in the morning, no matter how long the night has been, at midnight, another day begins. At sixty seconds after midnight, you are in a whole new day. Don't ever get stuck because of the tears. Don't ever think that your situation cannot change. There is another old gospel song that says, "I'm so glad troubles don't last always." You are going to have some "going through" in this life, but your situation is always subject to change.

REJOICE IN FAVOR

I once went to the store on a Saturday afternoon to buy some items for Christmas. My godson wanted some footballs and a Steelers jersey. I really wanted to get him what he'd asked for because his family had been through a lot that year, and I knew they might not have been able to get him anything. I am blessed to have so many connections and so much favor that I like to share my good fortune whenever I can. I ordered the jersey, and then I went to get the footballs. Not only was I blessed with one, but I was blessed with two NFL footballs. And I say that because I believe the favor that I received is directly due to my seeding in the spiritual realm (at my church). That favor, which is a gift from God, caused me to walk into a store where I got two items for the price of one. Favor will do that. When you seed in the spiritual, it will flow into the natural. Favor showed up for me in the market place, and now, with what I would have spent on the one person, I have more to bless someone else with.

Of course, we know that God's favor is unmerited because none of us deserves His favor. He gives that favor because of His grace, or He gives us favor because of who He is and what He wants to do. I believe that favor is part of the process of the sowing and planting that we have done. It is based on following the principles of God's Word that will cause favor to come upon your life.

God can do what He wants to do. He has mercy as He wills. He can choose to bless even those who do not serve Him, and He does. The Bible says, "For He maketh His Sun to rise on the evil and on the good, and sendeth rain on the just and on the unjust" (Matthew 5:45). In other words, God gives favor as He wishes; we don't "earn" it by our works. It is unmerited. We don't deserve it. We can't work for it. Instead, our trust and belief in God, coupled with our complete obedience to His Word and our desire to bless others *because* of His goodness to us, puts us in position to receive His favor.

In other words, as I mentioned earlier, when the seed (God's Word) is sowed in our lives (taught or preached to us), we want to be that good ground that takes the Word (seed) and believes it and allows it to change us for the better. Then, we seek to please God by sowing that same seed into other good ground. His favor is a miraculous blessing in whatever form it takes. Luke 1:28–30 describes when the angel of the Lord appeared to Mary, the mother of Jesus, and called her "highly favored" and stated that she had "found favor with God." She was chosen to carry the ultimate seed, the most precious seed: Jesus, the Son of God. He could have chosen anyone, but He chose Mary to favor with this divine assignment.

I know that I have so much favor because I believe. It is because of my heart and because I try to follow God's principles. I know it is unmerited favor, so when He blesses me, I turn around and bless someone else. I put my needs aside to help somebody else. I will put what I may want into someone else's hand because they are in need. I believe we should see the need and then help fill the need, whenever and wherever we can.

KEEP GOING

As I travel to the college in Wilmington, North Carolina, every year, I see these cornfields. Once, part of the field that I saw was just dirt. I went farther down the field, and I saw something coming toward me. As I got to the end, I saw a little harvest. So the process went through the stages to get to where I saw the end of it—the harvest. Coming back, I saw a man on a tractor starting the planting all over again. He was working to sow or plant something in order to reap what he had sown later on down the road. I am always blessed on this drive. This is something my coworker and I talked about as we traveled, and we were excited because the planting and harvesting gave us such an eloquent illustration of what I have been talking about in this book. A harvest starts out with nothing other than the seed that is planted in the dirt. I saw the farmer on the tractor with a field full of dirt, but when I got farther down the road, I saw what had grown from what the man started. Then, even farther down, I saw a field that was now in full harvest. And that is the process of the burial of the seed and the eventual rebirth as something greater.

The farmer had to plant, toil, and nurture, but he

knew that something was coming beyond that. I am pretty sure that he was looking beyond the dirt and planting with the expectation of growth. All that work that he put into this was going to be worth it later on down the road. Sometimes you have to look further ahead and see even before it comes, and that takes faith. Hebrews 11:1 says that "faith is the substance of things hoped for . . ." What am I hoping for? What are my expectations? "And the evidence of things not seen." Even though I don't see what I need or want with my physical eyes, I have to believe that it is there. My faith tells me that I see it.

It's a continual cycle. We're always planting, nurturing, and harvesting simultaneously. A farmer can't stop because farming is a way and means of life for him. Planting, nurturing, and harvesting is also a way and means of life for us, spiritually, as believers. When you look at ants, note that during the warm months, they constantly work, gathering food. They know that winter is coming, and they prepare so that when the season changes they will have what they need to survive until warmer weather returns. The process doesn't stop.

CONCLUSION

Never give up. Endure the process and know that it does get better. Always remember, if you help somebody out, somebody will help you in return. Remember, when you sow, do it with the right motive and the right heart. Good always will come to you. God will find a way to bless you. You may get blessed unexpectedly. Somebody that you may not know may help you.

A great example is Tyler Perry. When he was homeless, there was a lady standing behind him in line at the store, and she paid for his little snack. Twenty years later, out of the blue, he came across the same lady and found out her name. Perry learned that her house was in foreclosure, so he paid off her mortgage. She sowed something into this man's life twenty years before, and twenty years later—at the right time, the set time, the appointed time, the time of her need—she was remembered. Tyler remembered her, and he, in turn, sowed back into her life. Look at the reciprocity.

When you give, when you sow, when you plant, understand and know that at some point in time, that seed has to grow. It won't be easy, but it will be worth it. Prioritize your relationship with Christ and focus on your character. Know that anything that you're going through or have gone through is nothing new. Use those who have gone before you as a light. In addition to the many amazing biblical testaments, we also have more modern references to emulate. Maintain your thirst for knowledge, but don't be the type of person who learns but proceeds as if they don't know. It's critical that we not only hear God's Word, but that we model and teach it as well. How we teach it and to whom we teach it is unique; it is what makes you who you are. Spending precious time with God, embracing your gift, and not being afraid to speak about the goodness of God is how you discover your purposeful way of teaching the Word of God.

In addition to spreading His message, we also worship God through giving. How we give our time, our energy, and our money matters. Do so to the glory of God, to the best of your ability. Do so in excellence, knowing that a good name bears more weight than great riches. Remember, if you sow in greatness, then you'll harvest greatness as well. What's great varies from person to person. It depends on capability. And once you've done your part in sowing, know that you have a right to expect your harvest. Just as the seed fell on the good soil, there are those who, hearing the word, hold it fast in an honest and good heart and bear fruit with patience.

Waiting can be difficult, especially today when we're used to things coming to us so quickly. Stand in faith and stand firmly. This is part of getting into position and knowing who you are. For your entire life, you may have been told by others who you are and what kind of person you are. Your detractors don't have the last word, however. God does. And who does God say that you are? Who do you declare yourself to be? In 2 Corinthians 5:17, it says that anyone in Christ is a new creation. You may look like the same person, but you are not. Define for yourself who you are, what you stand for, and what you deserve.

Rejoice! Celebrate! We serve a mighty God! After everything that you've gone through, you're still here. That's favor. Take advantage of the breath in your body, and go forth and be great. Sow your seeds, understanding the power of the seed. Write down what you want your seed to do, and watch it come back to you, because it has to. God promised us that it would. Keep going. Continue the process all over, again and again and again. I pray that my life represents the power of believing. You have the authority, through Jesus Christ, to manifest anything you want, and your power to do so is no greater or smaller than the next person's. You just have to tap into it. Realize it and know. Activate the power of your seeds. Sow, nurture, and reap your harvest.

ABOUT THE AUTHOR

DR. ERIC L. HOLMES is a senior coordinator in the radiology department at Johns Hopkins Hospital in Baltimore, Maryland. His fervor to excel and push his abilities has led him to earn an impressive number of awards at Johns Hopkins: the Edward Halle Award, the Martin Luther King Award, the Radiology Customer Service Award, and Employee of the Year. With a passion and dedication to further his education and help others through his teachings, Dr. Holmes has earned a bachelor's and master's degree in biblical studies and theology, and a master's degree and doctorate in Christian education at the North Carolina College of Theology.

Dr. Holmes leads by example in everyday life by being a productive citizen and helping others in his community. Along with volunteering and participating in community outreach, Dr. Holmes loves to travel, read, and go to church.

You can connect with Dr. Holmes by emailing him at elynnk1306@gmail.com.

WE WANT TO HEAR FROM YOU!!!

If this book has made a difference in your life
DR. ERIC would be delighted to hear about it.

Leave a review on Amazon.com!

BOOK DR. ERIC TO SPEAK AT YOUR NEXT EVENT!

Send an email to: booking@publishyourgift.com

FOLLOW DR. ERIC ON SOCIAL MEDIA

 DrEricHolmes1

"EMPOWERING YOU TO IMPACT GENERATIONS"
WWW.PUBLISHYOURGIFT.COM

CPSIA information can be obtained at www.ICGtesting.com
Printed in the USA
BVOW01s1944050816

458084BV00008B/42/P